APRIL

little grief's hidden
in the bass of the skull split
can disappear now

briefs freeze the legs
in a cool chill on my haira
. HAIKU FOR SPRING

the muddy night bleeds
...rivers wash till morning comes
and the heart bleeds pain

Easter has roots here!
love rises from death Sundays
...siTHREE HAIKU

A big plate of fish
fried up to celebrate feasts
near the end of Spring

the moon looks hugely
down on our diming world now
the sun is old and tired

only the dead know
how much i love you, and how
deeply with hunger'

 WED HAIKU

the dim day lies down
....the sun and all its glory
sinks and gives us rest

lonely dogs roam now
...lost bitches in the alleys
give the night its hope

SIGNIFICANT HAIKU

big bold brassy nuts
...of the highest honor too!
...flashing for the world!

LIGHT HAIKU

a light difuses black
..it lathers the sky that way
...clouds spread like thunder

HAIKU FOR THE WARMTH

the nuts and nest warm
and days elongate further
...siesta past noon

INDIA HAIKU

the virus blossoms
....death bleeds into us always
...the spike is so real!

DAWN HAIKU

the calm of the day
is the morning twilight now
...summer shines for me

THURSDAY HAIKU

the stereo melts
into song and sings softly
morning songs to me

CLIMATE HAIKU

the planet will cool
...the carbon rate goes down now
,,,the species return

NUMBING HAIKU

frost covers me up
...mystical snows of my mind
...painlesss and cooling

love haiku

i sink into bed
hug my pillow like the niight
...think of you always

EMOTIVE HAIKU

fhe stroke took me up
...bloomed me...a shivering bum
....I lie awake nights

TWO SEX HAIKU

big arsed barbara
thighs around tight to my crotch
right in my two lips

the hills swim like her
woman of my dreams she was
...pastoral beauty

HAIKU WITH FRECKLES

when we are young girls
trapped in our minds in the dark
wondering the like

HAIKU FOR SOUTH

cane and cotton bloom
the eyes look white with red spots
...or far gone....downcast

MOVE HAIKU

traditions crumble
we go far and fast away
until we rest safely

SLUDGE HAIKU

muddy manners here
....the golden earth mixes up well
smells like earth and dung

COLD HAIKU

all night we shiver
surface of bodies to sheets
wishing we could hide

SWEET HAIKU

small as a handfull
big as a mountain as well
...the soul sweet i love

FALLING HAIKU

weakly plead mercy
from the abyss that fails you
deeply wounding life

STINKIN HAIKU

the anal canal
full of its crap and sex stuff
...hidden needs amass

SERANADE HAIKU

lilting notes expand
the universe unfolds so
...love is in the air!

RELIEF HAIKU

dead summer things end
in sweltering heat which lasts long
into the darkening

SOFT MUSIC HAIKU

religious notes sing
in choruses made to rember
...but so softly now

STICK HAIKU

stick like snake in mind
...is it stick or snake in mind
...only soul knows answere

GOD HAIKU

I need him alot
I am lost without him too!
Is the world ending?

MAMA GIRL HAIKU

the milk in the breast
and the gentley stroking look
...cushions for my head!

ANXIOUS HAIKU

nerves fire like bullets
the eyes swell redden alot
...love is suffuse now

CONFUSED HAIKU

confusion in mind
the hair stands electricly up
...everything is dumb

DRUNK HAIKU

drinking up the night
....a way to cream your brains up
in a toast to pride

HERO HAIKU

big balls and glory
fade with age to the uglies
...an old man sits, farts

LOVE DUST HAIKU

words full of sex now
...fill the void of our being
with the dust of peace

VIXEN HAIKU

rancid butter butt
...the lies she tells to move things
....they end up in hell

CHANGE HAIKU

my old self is gone
i am dumb but i am happy
watching things evolve

SOMEONES BIG HAIKU

rachel is perfect sweet
my hand trembles at her touch
sometimes she gets soft

PINCH ME HAIKU

its too good to be
so true it is....really great
i could float off too

CREAM HAIKU

the best of the fat
the thickest richest pornogragh
the real find you know

SUMMER ANXIETY HAIKU

you burn up real bad
but inside there is a sheer cool
frost outside where you gaze

COFFEE HAIKU

tastes delicious good
but it makes the heart race real fast
a little crazier

MOVING HAIKU

we make it away
we escape with breath to share
to a nice place there

BAD NERVES HAYKU

blood pressure soars up
talk gets messed up and confused
i want to sleep agatn

EMERGENCY ROOM HAIKU

all night you sweated
in a cold chair starving up
till you'd leave and die

MY HERO HAIKU

you stayed through hard pain
till they treated you...for me
and kitty you stayed

DOZING HAIKU

late at night music
plays with shinvers under fam
....in august heat here

MY APARTMENT HAIKU

no dusty corners
no room for desparing smudge
...just warm and cumfy

PHEONIX HAIKU

explosion to flame
in later years of living
where world ends like this

LINK HAIKU

line to line thingss join
in videos virtual real
light which lies to you

BIG SPACE HAIKU

the apartment has
room for sofas and artwork
and views of nature

LIVE HAIKU

rachel has to live
...enough of her medical hurt
....she must live and do well

SUMMER HAIKU

time to bake in sun
limp along decaying walkways
into a heater

RETIREMENT HAIKU

not from work but grief
stress does not sustain to well
...Hell is hot and cold

AIRCOOL HAIKU

the ice of the air
...artifice over heating
...silent illusion

NATURE ESCAPES ME HAIKU

so calming yet full
so alive with sex and hope
...perhaps it is false

VET CRAZY HAIKU

the cat howls in fright
his eyes dilate he sees fear
later falls asleep

TIME CRAZY HAIKU

we wait all in here
die during the minutes to
...the vet looks haggard

HOT HAIKU

the northwest has it
a swell of temperature
people cooked alive

WAKE UP HAIKU

do people not know
the earth is dying from heat
...surely now they know

TREES HAIKU

nature breathes, sweats rain
I am in awe by window
views of my garden

HAPPINESS HAIKU

please be happy now
we can manage our joy, art
kiss eternity

DISABLED HAIKU

i try to think, walk
help in small ways with leaving
but to no avail

THE SALE HAIKU

this huge house I love
...this relic of a small past
...away and gone now

LUCKY GUY hIKU

I was lukiest
when things fell apart. The world
baked like dough to bread

GNATS HAIKU

gnats swarm in the sun
the day is itchy rotten
the apple stinks too much

ELECTRIC RED HAIKU

the moon in autumn
turn to an orange balloon
in the hot fall sky

KNOW NOTHING HAIKU

what do we know now?
have we learned how to reason?
my head in the trash

FRAIL HAIKU

frail figures dance up
a storm for imagination
on the willow branches

END HAIKU

tiny end of living
in the space our embrace
...lucky man he was

WEIRD HAIKU

I am a limp dick
I am morally dirty
i am not myself

YOU HAIKU

pussies are hot too
be yourself when you love me
feel like dirt, lovely

TREADING WATER HAIKU

superficial steps
pushiing the walker this way
toward the hungry mail

LUCKY DAY HAIKU

frighterning...the miles
between the house and this place

....apartment in clouds

SHEIK HIKU

rubber bonnet on
the woman killer's helmet
....dying for allah

IDIOT HAIKU

presidential dumb!
big barbarian stupid
making fun of lame

flute haiku

jazz among the flat
apartments of chapel hill
blooming from the swamp

LYING HERE HAIKU

dreams sail by on clouds
love and sex sound like thunder
while you sink on down

RADIO TALK Haiku

the radio talks
the news is terrible but
also acurate

NEWS HAIKU

I stay awake now
listen to the news at night
and wonder things to

WASTE HAIKU

plastics abound here
all over the ocean too
they suffocate us

FALL HAIKU

I am heat tender
the sun bakes me bad these days
i sleep in aircool

BLOOD HAIKU

relation of genes
...hefty opening of veins
...early memory

INSECT HAIKU

six legged friendlies
...foreign in looks they seem like
but so alke they are

SUMMER BREEZE HAIKU

wafting lullibies
wake me to a bliue afternoon
dazzle me dreamy

INTINCT HAIKU

I have none, am mindless
but without a direction
....the chaos of the cosmos

the sickness haiku

my head is stuffed up
pain killers don't work that well
music and poems distract

SEPTEMBER HAIKU

frosty days creep in
in summer's elongation
to oblivion

HAUNT HAIKU

ghosts are coming here
they transcend form spacially
and quickly vanish

TWO HAIKU

morning frosted feilds
this way until winter arrived
bringing nighttime skys

the dark days come here
they swallow us alive too
coat everything darkly

TIRED OUT HAIKU

fatigue bleeds on us
...love is like that... it hurts you
we long for sleep now

BLUE MONDAY HAIKU

violons wept then
sunday turned to dry monday
on the radio

weekday haiku

Slpping through the week
mindlessly oblivious to
all of the things sinking

last haiku of the fall

the leaves don't shiimmer
...they bearly turn quite yellow
but the season is here

how precious the cold haiku

i dont want this burn
...this sweatshop of all the days
into a bleak future

EARLY FALL MORNING HAIKU

nothingness echoes
outside in the wind from us
here inside our thoughts

MENTAL NOTES OF COLD HAIKU

the planet warrms to fear
...the cold is not terrible
...the cold kiss of air

FEAR HAIKU

 i am paranoid
about the house selling wrongly
...so much at this hour

MOON HAIKU

the moon is the sign
of loves horrible falling
...so bleak and lonely

waft haiku

love laighs in Autumn
laughs with wind through leaves shaking
laughs and weeps a lot

SMALL SINS HAIKU

small sins make us sing
like humble dust amonga trees
we sing and laugh now

FALL HAIKU

leaf crisp! autumn bends
toward us is a wrinkled kiss
everything is good

COOL HAIKU

the cooling is great
the fall comes upon us now
Autumn is here

EMOTIONAL PAIN HAIKU

in love there is pain
there is a lightly blown breeze
in the autumn trees

EUINOX HAIKU

her love is immense
her coat sparkles up to us
autumn shivers up

stuck haiku

days shiver blandly
my anxiety terrifies me
i am stuck like glue

OLD CAT HAIKU

i am confronted
...a cat each time we argue
...old and tired...lumpy

WHOLE HEART HAIKU

I am your grin now
...what you laugh at knowingly
your eyes sparkling up

RELAXATION HAIKU

we had exploded then
into each others arms again
duribg a chilly fall

LATE IN LIFE HAIKU

we find then again
late in life love family
again we meamt them

SHIVERING DAWN HAIKU

corridors of light
suffuse the darkness early
with falls pronouncements

CHAPEL HILL HAIKU

your strangeness completes
my feelings of death inside
this strange twilight life

THE CHILL HAIKU

frost tingles today
the warming globe tilts spacewise
into the center

SHIVER HAIKU

i tremble at cold
the dead icicles drip down
the warmth is much worse

FRATRICIDAL RIGHTS HAIKU

pointing guns on black crowds
breathing poison breath iin food stores
without masked blockage

NERVOUS SLEEP HAIKU

up and down pacing
the hallways and corridors
of dreamless image

SHIVERING HAIKU

the cold comes in fall
lightly we tremble from cold
and the dark surrounds

SONG HAIKU

choral voices richly
sing the heart of us tonight
move like autumn leaves

WEEKEND HAIKU

Public Radio
plays music on the weekends

old timey good stuff

LIE IN BED HAIKU

listen to the best
news and music on the radio
not for money stuff

THE FROST OF DAWN HAIKU

silently cold comes
against the blues of friday
...love, lonely sinking

FALL MUSIC HAIKU

listen to the hard blues
of night in autumn freezing
love and lonely souls

FRATERNAL HAIKU

these labours last on
in the heart where they appear
in fall where they come

LONGING FOR SLEEP HAIKU

night will not last long
...that precious darkness ceases

that lovely numbness

THE NUMB HAIKU

in a kind of numb
end to us, the days warm up,
we doze off this way

ANXIETY HAIKU

chilled nuts in the pit
of the earthen stomuch seem
a normal thing now

FRIDAY BLISS HAIKU

muaic all evening
folk blues into the night now

lie in bed and sing

WEEKEND RADIO HAIKU

joy enourmous now
the night sings with the radio
...love is in the air

BARE FEET IN THE COLD HAIKU

I travel outside
stumble with my crippled legs
turn the lock clockwise
SHIVERING SIDEWAYS HAIKU

I am tired and cold
but i oerservere this way
come in to the light

THE SINS OF THE FATHERS HAIKU

we have ruined things
...the planet warns in bad ways
we sew a bad seed

RENEWAL HAIKU

things are getting good
slewly the effort is made
money where mouth is

QUIET RAIN HAIKU

pitter patter here
the slow drops of the season
lonely distant sound

NUMB AS DRUGS HAIKU

like the hospital
this quiet room in the rain
love waiting for death

YEARS PASS HAIKU

slow jazz meanders
so the river flows onward
dim llights capure us

LOVE IS SO HARD HAIIKU

nothing matters more

than that vast abyss wich calls
meeting likewise here

STARS FLOAT HAIKU

up there they float on
in the black heavens liike chalk
on a board etched there

LOVE IS BURNT HAIKU

love cooks in this heat
blisters with hot house sickness
in these, their final days

PORCH HAIKU

do you breathe in air
in the forest as i do
from my porch us there

DEATH HAIKU

black wood and black earth
in the forest of my dreams
as i fall asleep

THE COOL NIGHTS THAT COME HAIKU

terrible night comes
cold as ice our salvation
much like outer space

ROCK AND ROLL NIGHT HAIKU

this saturday night
will be bathed in music now
live rcck and roll plays

PRAYER HAIKU

god gives welcome here
blesses your meditation
on issues of peace

PRAYER 2 HAIKU

god liistens to us
our hearts are welcomed by him
inside of his arms

SHORT DAY HAIKU

frost snaps the branches
morning is hyonotic here

inside chapel hill

BREATHE IN HAIKU

breathe in the fall air
nuts adorn the yard these days
love sleeps eternally

THANKSGIVING HAIKU

this thursday along
with the poetry, stories
and the music too

THANK GOD HAIKU

thanks to the essence
we celebrate earth nature
along with good things

FIVE am HAIKU

at this blackenwd hour
where thunder stalks outside
...the deep muffled shade

WIND HAIKU

vague distances here
....music like tin ratling sad
...the humming sleeps now

CRIPPLE HAIKU

the limbs strain to walk
..ache in throbbing srides along
the pathways of fall

SIGNATURE HAIKU

x mark the spot here
not an x but a sleppy
zero on the line

SIGN YOUR NAME HAIKU

...but what is a name?
an indicator of my
presence here on earth

STOLEN HAIKU

fleeced by midnight's swirl
...stolen by the magnitude
of blackness late night

VINEGAR HAIKU

your cunt smells so good
...pregnant with the itch of dawn
...flowers of the bath

DISAPPEAR HAIKU

we will disappear
not from cold but too much warmth
into vacant space

MOUNTAIN HAIKU

winter mountain top
...cabin built and steaming up
...deer chassing shadows

LOVE NEEDS YOU HAIKU

love needs you like god
needs you in fear of years
needs you tomorow

WONDERFUL COOL HAIKU

the wonderful cool
of late fall into winter
...time to stare in awe

DROWSY FROST HAIKU

the frost is sleepy
it is cold and dark and dead
at this time of night

NUTS INDOORS HAIKU

crazy people sleep
at this time of night they sleep
and wake worrying

SPONGE LAND HAIKU

this swampy land mass
grown up to hills and valleys
flooding the tar heel

WATER HAIKU

the diluge and drip
of drizzle and stormy wet
weather upon us

THE DYING GRASSLANDS HAIKU

the grasslands die
dry up to poweder for desert
and the land so starves

WATER ASLO HAIKU

the slow incursion
of water upon the land
when glaciers melt

DYING OCEANS HAIKU

so small is essesnce!
everything breathing to eat
is so small for us

OUR VANITY DIM MISAKE HAIKU

such pitiful pride!
such sore stupidity stumbling
on a hapless cliff

SUCH A STRANGE STAR HAIKU

such a strange orb..us
we live or die...a flicker!
so easily snuffed

APPROACHING WINTER HAIKU

winter comes closer
with its deadly cold nighttimes
for all sick seasons

WINTER HAIKU

winter in two days
the dead fact of night drolls on
in frdgid silence

YOUR SLEEP HAIKU

your sleep is profound
dream invisiblle notions
in your minds eyes, ears.

COUPLES HAIKU

i look at you late
see your ancient curves at night
where breath rises and falls

CHRISTMAS EVE HAIKU

looking dow starry nights
to the mangy place where god
is born for us all

AT CHRISTMASS HAIKU

at this yule dawn fly

fly with morning wings on fire
be summer heart's desire

THE SCABS OF YEARS HAIKU

old sores on my legs
flake off as i scratch at them
old man sitting slow

CALIFORNIA RAIN HAIKU

its been wet winter
weather this year in the north
and we all stay on

RATIONING HAIKU

war years diet now
pennies spent for ticket food
and chickoree broth

HUNGRY DOG HAIKU

the pack steers toward scraps
...piles of skin and veggie broth
fishing tthrough the trash

CLIMATE DEPRESSION HAIKU

the legislation
fails for internet bullshit
...lemmiings we are now

CLIMATE DEPRESSION 2 HAIKU

depressing to live
on a futureless planet
countiing down the days

CHRISTMAS HAIKU

the center of us
born in december of the year
huddled and holy

NEW YEARS HAIKU

 new year approaches
it is hugely dauntingly
coming warmed all up

CHRISTMAS IS GONE HAIKU

I still hear carolls
on the computer awhile
...listen late at night

FROST HAIKU

in carolina
snows not that common these days
...just frosty mornings

FRUCTOSE HAIKU

bite into fruit and suck
or drink the essence also
...pears give up their stuff

SUCROSE HAIKU

sick headaches from sweets
....drinks oozing sugar that way
anxiety too

FIRE HAIKU

devastaton comes
heaves of smoke and ash also
breathlessness...eyes sting

TORNADO HAIKU

roofs torn and flying
debris throiugh air everywhere
noise like thunder clouds

JANUARY HAIKU

the dark days fallow
christmas and the new year too
off a cliff of warmth

WARM WINTER HAIKU

the year is warming
chaos fallows....storms and fires
...i love this world too

AFTER CHRISTMAS HAIKU

day of the christ child
ceases to be central now
...all things..subnormal

AFTER NEW YEARS HAIKU

post january
the world starts to stink again
....plegdes forgotten

LUKE WARM HAIKU

the first snow came then
melted quickly...disappeared
...our ghost of an earth

THE RICH HAIKU

Maybe businessmen
will save us..surely they would
rather not die also.

LATE MORNING HAIKU

daylight creeps inside
this swamp of smaller city
of the south u.s.

WINTER TIREDNESS

i am lost within
the grey fatigue of winter
in carolina

STRANGE MUSIC HAIKU

strange passion i can't
remove without dying from it
....addiction of the heart

MY OTHER HAIKU

she is the essence
of my heart..the thing i want
strangely all the time

STUPID ME HAIKU

after the stroke comes
so the fog of mind coats me
my brain..dully done

FIRE GAME HAIKU

the fire ignites them
then subsides to ashes gone
planetary ash

RAIN ON FIRE HAIKU

its strange the way it
rained on our sweltering heat
this bad time of year

CALIFORNIA SONG HAIKU

the west coast...victum
of our predatory past crime
of pollution too

CHRIST OF COLD HAIKU

shivering in our
anguished church pews at late night
the years came to this

SUB ZERO HAIKU

things get cold as well
the climate is unstable
and the stiorms come too

SUCH A SWEET PLACE TO LIVE HAIKU

sweet place to live in
this chapel hill nook nc
such a sweet winter

SUCH A SWEET PLACE TO FALL ASLEEP HAIKU

such a sweet place here
lying in my lovers arms
late winter evenings

FEAR IN THE DARK HAIKU

a kind of numbness
...a sick lonely fear, relieved
to oblivion

HIDING IN THE DARK HAIKU

shivering under sheets
squinting to dream in the night
while the earth goes sour

WINTER MORNING HAIKU

sunlight breaks early
sprinkles snowy vibrance here
in the dawn valley

SOFT LIGHT HAIKU

sunlight through window
warms the dawn in weary ways
.....back to sleep with you

ELECTRIC CAR HAIKU

who would have thought that
ceos at ford and gm would
would be the vanguard

A STRANGE TIME HAIKU

businessmen are not
crazy like republicans are
to sell destruction

QUIET PLACES HAIKU

nothing sounds in here
in the depth of my morning
nothing disturbs the heart

FROZEN PLACES HAIKU

love is asleep in its
refrigerator ease, now
love is calmly good

VAENTNE HAIKU 1

slipping toward the frost
of midfebruary's shoe
skating toward light love

VALENTINE HAIKU 2

kisses meet the cold
the air swells with its loving
pregnant with desire

VALENTINE HAIKU 3

we dash into wood
ripe with love's february
full of tomorow

VALENTINE HAIKU 4

kisses in the cold
love in frozen season
sweet and shivering

VALENTINE HAIKU 5

our tongues stick with love
i will always follow you
you are everything

PUTIN'S WAR HAIKU

he's going to burn
the whole place down on us
getting even too

SANCTIONS HAIKU

they are not an act
of war. they stop a war too.
these are trying times

MY RACHEL HAIKU

my rachel, my heart
my heaven and dream of old
beauty like yoor art

LOVE LIKE GLUE HAIKU

love that sticks the heart
onto the seasons of years
of your blue green eyes

DEEP YEARNING HAIKU

what i want is you
deeply in the gut i want
be with you now

BARRIERS HAIKU

something comes between
....there is always some block here
in our flow of hearts

STILL WINTER HAIKU

winter is still cold
...even with the warming world
we shiver these days

FAT ROBBIN HAIKU

the colosus of
spring in miniature days
hides at winter's end

FAT ROBBIN 2 HAIKU

so small are these days
at the end of winter now
huge, the spring to come

STEVE ALIVE HAIKU

steve computer whiz
giant of data process
our bright extinct age

LYNN SHARE HAIKU

pain and anxiety
over the telephone line
step by step resolved

IN THE FLOOD OF SPRING HAIKU

the chilled rain flowing
down the embankment and on
...a mark of hesitance

SHIVERING IN THE HEAT HAIKU

i stll shiver these days
even with the warming here
...there is no place else

WORRYING HAIKU

at last the spring comes
warm but somehow anxious too
...the buzz of the town

FIRST DAY OF SPRING HAIKU

god sings to the heart
in mornings full of our tears
at night soft songs come

EVEN WITH CLIMATE CHANGE HAIKU

the days are still flush
with shivering spring again
the days go cooly

STUPID ME HAIKU

i stumble these days
wait stupidly to die here
happy i am now

UNLUCKY SPRING HAIKU

the days pass from dawn
till the music of nighttime
i hum poems waiting

THE MARROW BLEEDS TO SEED HAIKU

waking slowly now
a third time in the morning
over a cup of brew

SPRING LULLABY HAIKU

the days warn slowly
even now from chill to heat
the porch is stunning

MARCH 25TH HAIKU

the warm sunlight creeps
through morning portals it flows
to the forest floor

LOVE AND NATURE

these broken twigs show
the rustic signs of my heart
...my love is wooded

COUNTRY GIRL HAIKU

you are sweetest song
heart of the farm and forest
for you i live, die

SPRING SINGS SILLY HAIKU

hear the water lap
the shores of the melted lake
....with only kisses

BRSK LOGIC HAIKU

one step at a time
toward where the bottom leads to
at the end of it

BRISK NONSENSE HAIKU

walk rapidly nowhere
on nothingness crazy sore
with memories gone

SPRING SHIVERS HAIKU

early dawn we wake
the sunlight creeps upon us
outside the porch door

WINDMILLS HAIKU

windmills make movement
for power from the ocean
far out in the waves

THE PROBLEM HAIKU

i was born wrongly
some part of me was dumb then
...unable to speak

WHAT STRANGE THING HAIKU

what strange thing was it?
that caused my collapse these years
...strange thing forgotten

I AM HAPPY HAIKU

i am happy now
live well with my confusion
in this strange country

THE TRAGIC HEART LAUGHS HAIKU

here in old age laugh
like us god laughs just as well
all night by the fire

EACH BLADE OF GRASS HAIKU

life and death in each
in each stringy blade of grass
...stand up and laugh now

JOY HAIKU

music and nature
fill the world the trees, oceans
flood my heart with love

DESCENT HAIKU

down we went enjoined
to the basement of our love
to stare at ourselves

FRONTAL LABOTOMY HAIKU

as i age dull mind
i grow pacific inside
...waddle in the sun

WE SMILE ACHING HAIKU

laughter falls upon us
with our pain...is part of age
this way of our lives

PUSHING LIKE NAKED SPRING HAIKU

root to bud this time
innocent and stubbornly

i fallow downward

THE STUPID WAYS WE LOVE HAIKU

simple and singular
dully straight toward your heart
i give you my gift

STILL SHIVERIG HAIKU

winter keeps a cold
eye on the paths that i take
blows to let me know

the whole mad swirl of everything to come begins now!

   What's New
   Poetry Forum
   Short Stories
   Mad Gallery
   Open Mic
   Submissions

Sam Silva

LYNN SHARE HAIKU
featured in the poetry forum March 27, 2022 :: 0 comments

pain and anxiety
over the telephone line
step by step resolved

editors note:

Everyone is looking for a Lynn to lighten the load. – mh clay
2 Haiku: THE FROST OF DAWN & TREES
featured in the poetry forum January 16, 2022 :: 0 comments

THE FROST OF DAWN

silently cold comes
against the blues of friday
...love, lonely sinking

***

TREES

nature breathes, sweats rain
I am in awe by window
views of my garden
editors note:

Outer spaces spur inner graces. – mh clay
Three Haiku: Sale, Lucky, Gnats
featured in the poetry forum October 21, 2021 :: 0 comments

THE SALE

this huge house I love
...this relic of a small past
...away and gone now

***
LUCKY GUY

I was luckiest
when things fell apart. The world
baked like dough to bread

***
GNATS

gnats swarm in the sun
the day is itchy rotten
the apple stinks too much
editors note:

Just as life comes in short bursts; our luck can turn on the sale of a gnat. – mh clay
LIGHT HAIKU

featured in the poetry forum July 19, 2021 :: 0 comments

a light diffuses black
..it lathers the sky that way
...clouds spread like thunder
editors note:

A light lather is a close shave. – mh clay
FRANKENSTEIN
featured in the poetry forum April 30, 2021 :: 0 comments

Places where the dead are plugged
...electric to all passion's core
wandering the peasant groves
...confused by an uncertain brain
and terrorizing man and beast
and women also
like a boar
searching warmth
in fear of fire.
Destruction in desire's feast
the way the dead can feel desire!!
editors note:

Like this, we grope our grove, in search of life's bright bolt. – mh clay

LIVING AMONG THE MIDDLE CLASSES
featured in the poetry forum February 2, 2021 :: 0 comments

An achy nervousness
among pandemic days
while summer turns toward Fall
and the politics of madness

in the election of it all

and my own old age decays
dully for its sadness
like some disease which slays

with a sleep that fills our eyes
with an image on TV
of dreamy dreamy hot fires
in the skies.
editors note:

Flat screen, flat deal! We are what we watch. – mh clay

THE LOVE BOND
featured in the poetry forum November 7, 2020 :: 0 comments

See we are ancient already! We are marble
carved and sealed to fortressed stone
inseparable the way we aged together
and glistening in our polish
like one of your starry paintings.

Or an old rustic house
grown out as one toward the woodland.

We live in the same skin
shelter under each other's locks.

I look out the window of your brilliant eyes
and see and give utterance for the world
eternally brand new!
editors note:

Yes! Give utterance! – mh clay
THE FAILED ARTIST
featured in the poetry forum August 17, 2020 :: 0 comments

Nature's first rule is predation
a fact in the face
which he could not stand

so he puffed up a cloud
in his glacial station
to obscure that cruel beauty
of the land.
editors note:

In this case, smoke 'em when you DON'T… – mh clay

ART AS THE GHOSTLY SOPRANO
featured in the poetry forum June 15, 2020 :: 0 comments

This is the love among the dead
…these are those high operatic notes
…that gorge of meat and wine and bread
…that private castle leaking hope, despair,
the two the same in desperate sighs

encased in predatory motes

to keep away the warlike herds
of Mongols milking mares and goats
with lost dreams much like lullabies
composed by angels

….without words…
editors note:

And, yet, we must sing them… – mh clay
THE MUSIC OF THE OCEAN'S COAST
featured in the poetry forum April 10, 2020 :: 0 comments

Midnight longing for God and Heaven
Horns of sweet jazz for Jesus
in the missionary night.

Converting bats like me to bliss,
bugs, to that kiss of divinity
…the lucky and beloved to a sigh
alike the sea
editors note:

Sing contentment in every key. – mh clay

1
2
3
?

A bit about Sam: Sam Silva has poetry in print magazines including, but not limited to Samisdat, The ECU Rebel, Sow's Ear, The American Muse, St. Andrews Review, Dog River Review, Third Lung Review, Main St. Rag, Charlotte Poetry Review, Parnasus...most (but not all) of these magazines are now defunct. For the past four years his magazine portfolio has grown by and large on line including Rio Del Arts, Megaera, Big Bridge, Views unplugged, Comrade Magazine, Ken Again and at least thirty others. Over the years four small presses have published a total of nine chapbooks by Sam Silva ...these, being Third Lung Press, M.A.F. Press, Alpha Beat Press, Trouth Creek Press. Brown and Yale Universities solicited many of these chapbooks for their libraries. These chapbooks were well received in newspaper reviews by Shelby Stephenson, Ron Bayes, Steve Smith, and the late poet laureate of North Carolina Sam Ragan. Silva has ebooks available without cost at Physikgarden.com. He has well over 300 poems archived in online magazines. He was nominated a total of seven times by three small presses and has a full length collection of poetry called Eating and Drinking based on a royalties contract signed with Bright Spark Creative available for order at any online bookstore and has other full length poetry books

available at amazon.com. Three spoken word CDs of Sam Silva's have been marketed through CDBaby.
What's New

Poetry
  Short Stories
  Mad Gallery
  Open Mic
  Submissions
  Contact
  Merch

© 2022